PgMP Latest Certification Exam Study Guide:
Practice Questions and Answers to pass the Program
Management Professional Certification Exam

Maverick Braylon

COPYRIGHT

PRACTICE QUESTIONS AND ANSWERS

Question 1

Your platform has 121 partners with which you will have to connect. The Communications Management Strategy outlines how correspondence should take place, message that should be conveyed, and the planned communication modality. Would you still need require one of the mentioned below as a contribution to the method of dissemination of information in your program?

A. Requests for Improvement

B. Won outcomes in performance control

C. Reports on results

D. Analysis strategy for stakeholders

Answer: D

Question 2

What is the method used by a program to evaluate earned value (EV)?

A. Percent full period at conclusion of the service budget

B. Percentage completes period calculating the program

cost

C. The number of full cycles remaining in the curriculum

D. Percent total times the expense of labor as well as supplies of the program

Answer: A

Question 3

Olive is her organization's program planner. She also produced a suggestion request for a significant quota of her curriculum. She has fixed some conditions for the sellers to engage in this task to be obtained. The chief of these conditions is that a dealer must have in his staff minimum of four accredited electricians. For 4 accredited electricians, this criterion is an instance of which one of the following terminologies?

A. Criteria of Assessment

B. Model of Scoring

C. Requirements for Vendor review

D. Method of screening

Answer: D

Question 4

For a particular company, you are the program planner. Administration has told you to develop a paper that will grip the fears, potential risks and concrete priorities of the initiative and its programs of the investors. In this case, what document is the administration asking you to produce?

A. document requirements

B. Scope statement

C. Project contract

D. commercial case

Answer: B

Question 5

As an NHQ Program manager for a particular program. To make sure that the job in the curriculum is completed correctly and as regards to the scope, you are collaborating alongside the program staff.

You are also evaluating the method of team inspection that would need to be conducted to make sure that the job is completed according to the scope. It would have to be fixed if the work is discovered to be faulty prior the program consumers can check the work. To ensure that the job is completed regarding to the scope, what phase are you implementing?

A. Quality control

B. Preparation

C. Scope Authentication

D. Quality assurance

Answer: D

Question 6

A teaming partnership for an opening has been established between your company and a rival company. You as well as your opponent will complete a big initiative for a customer with this team arrangement. For all organizations, this is, theoretically, a risk retort. In this case, what sort of risk retort/response are you transacting with?

A. Grouping

B. Sharing

C. Manipulating

D. Tolerant

Answer: B

Question 7

A project manager has projected the price of a service in your program to be 145,000 dollars. The project manager discovers that he only has $27,876 remaining in his project account, as the project manager's task is near to completion. In an effort to use the leftover budget, he wanted to include some new functions to the project's output. These additions would bring importance to the project plus these additional attributes are likely to be appreciated by the project customer. This is an instance of what terminology?

A. Plating of gold

B. Mistakes and Errors

C. Expert decision by the founder of the project

D. Quality Shift applied

Answer: B

Question 8

Jade is the HQN Task's program manager. This program is closing to its end and the job's budget only has $25,000 left. Jade requested the task team to find any new deliverables that may be utilized in the framework of the program to boost the output of the job, however also to utilize all the budget funds. In this case, what word is allocated to the behavior that Jade is trying to do?

A. Requests for Value-added shift

B. Zero Budgeting Based

C. Integrated regulation of transition transitions

D. Plating of gold

Answer: D

Question 9

What form of study should you utilize in a program to equate the positive investors with similar variable modules of the negative investors in your program and their role, control, and impact on your program?

A. Analyzing sensitivity

B. Analysis of stakeholders

C. Simulation of Monte Carlo

D. Force arena evaluation

Answer: D

Question 10

Having appoint you as the manager of the BHG Service program. Using new products that are very untested would be one of the tasks in your curriculum. You are worried that delays as well as waste can occur due to the project members is unsure of how to utilize these resources correctly. Via instruction on ways to finish their project task, you plan to submit the people who will utilize the new materials. Before the real project task is to be completed, you even encourage them to buy few of the materials to play for their use. You want to ensure that errors are not portion of the project. In this case, what type of intervention did you provide?

A. Here is quality assurance case.

B. This is an instance of the growth of teams.

C. This is an instance of a precautionary measure.

D. It is an instance of remedial intervention.

Answer: C

Question 11

In a renowned organization, you are the program planner. You as well as the program staff developed and passed the advantages of the program to activities as possible in the implementation of the program. What method of program administration represents the procedure of achieving the advantages of the program?

A. Aids management

B. Quality control

C. QA

D. Guide and control execution of program

Answer: D

Question 12

What is the current worth of a $3,567,000 program if it runs for six years then the return factor is 5%?

A. 1,550,850 dollars

B. 3,532,000 dollars

C. 2,502,750 dollars

D. 2,661,750 dollars

Answer: D

Question 13

In regards to the SRQ Program, you are assigned to be the program manager. For the program outlines, you have declined multiple modification requests. What exactly do you need to fix with the denied demands for change?

A. Communicate that the recommendation for reform was denied and report the findings in the documentation of the lessons learned for the curriculum.

B. Notify the investors that their applications for reform have been denied.

C. Tell investors that their applications for reform have been denied.

D. Inform them about the progress of the change proposal to the investors and report the result of the request for change in the modified register.

Answer: D

Question 14

Negative hazard documented are _____?

A. Negative hazard register

B. Hazard administration plan

C. Problem log

D. Hazard register

Answer: D

Question 15

For a specific company, you are the program planner. For your initiative, management would prefer to understand the current benefit. If the program is projected to be valued at $450,000 in 2 years, what is the program's current value if the interest rate is 6%?

A. $385,450 dollars

B. 400,498 dollars

C. $505,620

D. 521,345 dollars

Answer: B

Question 16

Stella is the PM of a wide company and in her company has a high profile as well as popularity. Some of the investors are negative, also to resolve their worries, supposed risks, including their concerns as regards the initiative, Stella wants to collaborate with these investors. For this case, which negotiation strategy is perceived to be the best method?

A. One on many

B. Many-to-several people

C. Conversation ad hoc

D. Face-to-face

Answer: D

Question 17

John is the NQQ Project manager and has recruited the ZAS Company to finish part of Eric's organization's project work. Due to an order for improvement, the ZASS

Since almost all of the project task has been done, the firm is no longer wanted for the task. Is John's company responsible for paying the ZAS Organization for the task on the project they have done so far?

A. It depends on what the contract's termination clause stipulates.

B. No, much of the work was not done by the ZAS Company.

C. It is subject to what a lawsuit's outcome will decide.

D. Yeah, the ZAS Company did not intend to cancel the job under the contract.

Answer: A

Question 18

Mike who is the NHQ Task's program manager. Mike as well as a vendor disagree with the vendor's deliverables produced for Mike's program. Mike doesn't accept that the supplier has adequately delivered the deliverable, whilst the supplier is confident that the order has already been fulfilled by his firm. In the controversy, both sides have taken note of their position.

This is an instance of _____?

A. contract breach

B. Claim

C. Dispute

D. Hazard

Answer: B

Question 19

In your company, you are assigned as GHY PM. It has come to your notice that in order to pad their periods in situation whereby any incident occurs in their project that will lead to delays, certain project managers in your platform are adding time to every single project activity. What principle do you share with these PM's who with extra time counteract the notion of padding activities?

A. Pareto's Law

B. The Diminishing Returns Theorem

C. Law 80/20

D. Law of Parkinson's

Answer: D

Question 20

You are assigned as the program planner of an organization. There are 43 persons in your program team that needed to be tracked and managed. You would like to develop a structured report that can be utilized in the curriculum to track, manage, and document the success of each of the team members. What type of report will you generate that will assist you track your employees and their performance?

A. Reports of workers variation

B. Reports on performance

C. Report of Exceptions

D. Learned Lessons

Answer: B

Question 21

For a repeatable mechanism in your program, you have developed a control map. You also noted that in your monitoring table, the seven most recent measurements are all on the positive side of the average. What do they call this phenomenon?

A. Regulation of Improvement

B. Mean Enhancement

C. Rule of Seven

D. Low -Equestrian Mean

Answer: C

Question 22

What portion of the change management framework is responsible for the assessment, testing and documentation of the project scope changes created?

A. Knowledge Method in Project Management

B. Integrated Monitoring of Improvements

C. Assurance of Scope

D. Alignment Management structure

Answer: D

Question 23

Donna is her organization's project manager. She is

preparing a roadmap to handle project improvements should amendments be required. The mechanism for recording, monitoring, and deciding whether the modifications should be accepted or rejected is specified by her change management strategy. What system is considered the parent of the system of change control recorded in the plan of Donna?

A. Framework for Quality Control

B. Adjust Regulator System

C. Project Management Info System

D. Centralized Framework for Change Management

Answer: C

Question 24

For the company, you are a program planner. You also recommended a management curriculum that would last four years and cost $35 million to build. Management also asked to see the charter of the program and the program's suggested expenses and benefits.

Management commits to the charter of your program and offers to finance the program at the end of each milestone in installments. What kind of financing is being proposed by the management for this program?

A. Cautious

B. Step financing

C. Breakthrough approval

D. Stage gate appraising

Answer: B

Question 25

You're the HYH Program Admin. Your governance of the program allows you to use earned benefit management to predict how tightly the expense and plan baselines are tracked by your program and to predict overall program performance. Based on current program results, what earned value management model will you use to determine how much more would need to be spent in the program?

A. AC/EV

B. EA/PC

C. CIP/BCA

D. EAC-AC

Answer: D

Question 26

For the organization, you are the program planner. Who would need to sign the certificate of completion when a project in your program is finished?

A. The head of the project

B. customer program

C. Stakeholders in the program

D. The project development committee

Answer: B

Question 27

For the organization, you are the program planner. As the program manager, part of the job is to educate John, a new program manager, on the program processes inside a program. John is uncertain about where in the program management lifecycle the program team will be acquired. When can the program team for a program be acquired?

A. Scheduling

B. Execution

C. Observing and regulatory

D. Instigation

Answer: B

Question 28

For the organization, you are the program planner. You are now collaborating with Nancy Holmes, the program director, to identify a new program and the advantages that can be generated by the program. What of the above is the better description of a profit that a program produces?

A. A profit is a result of a scheme of the constituent projects.

B. A advantage is a schedule and service deliverables that can be used directly by the company.

C. A profit is a program or initiative deliverable that is worth more than the cost to produce the deliverable.

D. A benefit is a product of attitudes and attitudes that give stakeholders value.

Answer: D

Question 29

For your company, you are the program manager and you need to identify all the program tools you may need for your program. All of the above, but this one, should be called a program resource?

A. A Forklift

B. Materials for a new server installation

C. A positive hazard reply

D. Gary, a developer of apps

Answer: C

Question 30

Your program has been chosen and it is now establishing a program charter. All of the following features are specified by the program charter, except for which one?

A. Constraints of the curriculum

B. Scope of program

C. For the curriculum, high-level priorities

D. Statement of project reach for all the programs inside the program

Answer: D

Question 31

Terri is her organization's program planner, and she partners with Alice, her program's project manager. Alice phones Terri, demanding that she add a modification to the scope of the curriculum. Terri acknowledges that there should be an entertaining improvement. What would Alice need to do to go on with her call for change?

A. Add the adjustment to the scope of the program itself, since she is a project manager,

B. Add the proposal for improvement to the scope and full integrated oversight of the change

C. In a change request type, log the change request.

D. Establish a charter of change proposal explaining the change request

Answer: C

Question 32

For the NHQ Program, you are the program manager.

Your system has a budget of

4,500,000 dollars and it lasted for two years. Your program has just reached its last deliverable, and the final closure processes of the program are being completed. What paperwork does the recipient of the program sign now as part of the termination of the program?

A. The program scope must be signed by the client now.

B. The bill for the program work must now be signed by the recipient.

C. The customer must sign the program termination certificate now.

D. The organizational transition agreement must be signed by the client now.

Answer: C

Question 33

You are the YGH Program manager. For your scheme, a vendor has recently finished his contracted job. You accept that the procured work has been done by the supplier, but what paperwork do you and the suppliers sign now?

A. Completion certificate

B. Offer contract

C. Bill

D. Deal

Answer: A

Question 34

For the organization, you are the program planner. Management has requested that you decide when services are no longer necessary, such as rented facilities, so that you can unlock the resources inside the program to save time, money, and usage of resources. What process of program management is leadership asking you to perform?

A. Bond administration

B. Supply administration

C. Resource control

D. Procurement control

Answer: C

Question 35

Molly is her organization's event planner. She is producing a guide that outlines the savings that the program can provide after the program has been completed for her company. What paper is being written by Molly?

A. Program approval

B. Program aids realization proposal

C. Program agenda plan

D. Program benefits statement

Answer: C

Question 36

For the organization, you are the program planner. Management is considering a new initiative, but they are concerned about the dangers of the program that may impact the effectiveness of the program.

You recognize that there are three reactions to positive risks and three reactions to negative risks that each risk can have. Management asks you which risk answer would be more fitting if they chose to employ a third party to own the risk event for the program with a big risk event. Which danger case is most suitable?

A. Evasion

B. Justification

C. Transference

D. Distribution

Answer: C

Question 37

For the organization, you are the program planner. For 17 potential vendors, you have produced a statement of work, a request for proposal, and an invitation to a bidder's meeting. Questions regarding your proposal request and declaration of work were posed during the meeting, leading to clarifications. After the vendor meeting, what data can you change to give back to the vendors?

A. Application for bid records

B. Submissions

C. Job description

D. Management strategy for the initiative

Answer: C

Question 38

You are the project manager for the organization and collaborate with the partners of the project and the business consultant to identify all the deliverables to be generated by the project. The stakeholders would like the chance later in the project to add more deliverables to leave the specifications relatively open for modifications. You demonstrate to the organization analyst that you need a series of criteria that specify precisely what the project wants to be delivered. In this early phase of the project, what paper are you trying to create?

A. Technical evidence Specifications

B. Statement of project scale

C. Charter of ventures

D. Project Paper in Depth

Answer: B

Question 39

For the HNQ Organization, a new initiative is being launched. To identify several features of the program, the program manager collaborates with the market analyst and management. During program initiation, all of the above are listed, except for which one?

A. Program hazard

B. Program advantages

C. scope plan

D. Relation to organizational policy

Answer: A

Question 40

As a program planner, you must also consider the life cycle of project management and the lifecycle of the project. What is the distinction between the two?

A. The lifecycle of project management and the project lifecycle are the same thing.

B. The life cycle of project management consists of initiating, preparing, implementing, tracking and managing, and closing stages. The lifecycle of the project includes stages that are specific to the work of the project.

C. The lifecycle of project management is specific to each project, although the life cycle of the project is universal for all projects.

D. The lifecycle of project management is universal for all projects and the lifecycle of the project is unique to each project.

Answer: D

Question 41

For the organization, you are the program planner. In the curriculum calendar, you are reviewing the order of the tasks and would like to adjust some of the order to eliminate scheduling problems, threats, and depending on your familiarity of the discipline used by the program. Some of the tasks you should schedule and some of the tasks need to be performed in a certain order. What word defines the tasks that can take place in any order?

A. Terminate on limits

B. Optional dependencies

C. Dependencies that are mandatory

D. Dependencies in benefits delivery

Answer: B

Question 42

For your company, you are the program planner and plan the tasks and duties of your program. For the program task, you would like to create a RACI graphic. What is said by RACI?

A. It is a list of roles and obligations that uses accountable, liable, advising, and informing responsibilities as the legend of the map.

B. It is a map of roles and obligations that uses the responsibilities of duty, intervention, consultation, and concern as the legend of the chart.

C. It is a map of roles and obligations that uses money, actions, contributions, and responsibilities as the legend of the chart.

D. It is a list of roles and obligations that includes responsibilities to be responsible, accountable, contribute and advise as the map legend.

Answer: A

Question 43

You are the manager of the OFE Program. To ensure that there is continuity in the delivery of the program schedule, you collaborate with the program team and project managers. You emphasize that the task has been scheduled and now the team has to complete the work correctly. The first time in the program, you want to know that the job is done appropriately. To the program team and project supervisors, what kind of method do you stress?

A. Quality assurance

B. Scope authentication

C. QC

D. Progression development

Answer: A

Question 44

You are the company's program manager and oversee and control many facets of your program. You want to make sure that all areas that need to be supervised and controlled are included. What one of the above isn't something that as a program manager you'll have to track and control?

A. Program-required materials

B. Stakeholder ID

C. In your program, Susan the Application Creator

D. Equipment used for the program

Answer: B

Question 45

The initiative has a completion budget of $1,250,000 and has only invested $425,000. Owing to some manufacturer delays, the program is running late; the program is just 30 percent complete, while at this point it was expected to be 45 percent. Based on this evidence, how much more money would it cost to complete this program?

A. 978,445 dollars

B. 919,325 dollars

C. 991,667 dollars

D. 987,544 dollars

Answer: C

Question 46

Your program has a $1,550,000 completion target that is

planned to run for one year.

Your program is now 45% complete, and $725,000 has been invested. You are actually going to be fifty percent complete by this time, according to the program schedule, but the program is running just a little late due to some vendor delays. Based on this worse-performing data, the cost or schedule?

A. The agenda is carrying out worse due to SPI is .90

B. Since the EAC is $1,611,111, the rate is getting worse.

C. The timetable is getting worse since the SV is -$27,500.

D. The price is worse, since the CPI is .96.

Answer: A

Question 47

Which of the above is not an aspect of the template designed to make the project more efficient?

A. Definition of the packages for work

B. Tools and abilities needed

C. Acts needed to complete the scope of the project

D. agreement file

Answer: D

Question 48

In your program, you mentor Tammy, a project planner, on the advantages of program management. She is stumped as to why you would create a package so that you can share all the rewards of a program with her. What of the above is an advantage of program creation?

A. In an enterprise, services often cost less than several initiatives.

B. The project control of the program manager is centralized.

C. Programs offer integrated risk management.

D. Management of the program enables coordination between the project administrators and the project staff.

Question 49

Identifying what motivates the members of the program staff is part of program management. If you belong to the Hierarchy of Needs of Maslow, who needs to be at the top of the hierarchy?

A. Functional

B. Security

C. Respect

D. Self-actualization

Answer: D

Question 50

Inside a matrix form, the program lives. There are eight initiatives in the curriculum that all pool capital from across the organization. You are worried that any of the members of the project team could be over-allocated and want to construct a map that represents resource usage. What kind of map would illustrate the usage of members of the project team used in your program?

A. Network diagram for services

B. Structure of Resource Breakdown

C. Reserve histogram

D. Map Pareto

Answer: C

Question 51

The Robert program is sliding on its timeline, and management has asked Robert to find a way to compress the program's length. If he applied labor to the effort-driven operations inside the program, what strategy could Robert take that would not significantly add risks to the program?

A. Main time

B. Fast tracking

C. Interval time

D. Crashing

Answer: D

Question 52

When it comes to policy modification demands for the program scope, which of the following points is the most precise?

A. The timetable must not be influenced by the order for adjustment.

B. The proposal for a modification does not impact the

total rate.

C. The program's consistency must not be compromised by the order for a modification.

D. The modified demand must be noted.

Answer: D

Question 53

You are identifying partners to develop new program for your company for your program. The program can influence consumer purchasing, product manufacturing, inventory, and account management. Sarah, a key stakeholder in the initiative, is suspicious of too many areas of the company being influenced by one application. Instead of the approach your program would take, she recommends that many applications be developed.

How can you identify Sarah in terms of stakeholder identification?

A. Dynamic

B. Negative

C. Positive

D. Consistence

Answer: B

Question 54

Marty is the project director for the recently ended NHK Project. The project client found the project satisfactory and they signed the formal approval documents. Marty wrote the final project summary, released the project team, and finalized the analysis of the lessons learned. What else can Marty do as the NHK Project shuts down?

A. Summarize the difference in the project.

B. Archive archives of a project.

C. Summarize the costs of project risks.

D. Lock the office for the project.

Answer: B

Question 55

Which of the following points regarding the vital route is most precise?

A. The route that displays the length of the project is indeed the crucial path.

B. There is no float on the vital track.

C. As it has the most operations, the vital path is the longest path.

D. The vital route indicates which route has the highest chance of failure.

Answer: B

Question 56

You are the manager of the program for the BHN Program. Your initiative has 122 partners with which you would need to prepare to engage. How many lines of contact do you have in this program, given the complexity of the program?

A. 244

B. 7,381

C. 12, 676

D. 814

Answer: B

Question 57

You are the HNG Program Manager. This program has a $2,345,900 completion budget that is intended to run for two years. At present, the program is 30 percent complete and you have invested $789,000. The program is expected to be 35% complete, but you are slightly behind schedule with some delays. What is the schedule variance (SV) of this program based on this information?

A. -$95,250

B. $921,055

C. -$117,295

D. -$217,655

Answer: C

Question 58

Any of the above documents offers the order to implement the initiative under a certain timeframe and often provides targets or cumulative rewards for the distribution of products?

A. Platform planning baseline

B. Platform risk record

C. Program charter

D. WBS program

Answer: C

Question 59

Which of the following procedures is the charter for the program formed?

A. Establish a financial system program

B. Plan Scope of the Curriculum

C. Launch Program

D. Develop a Plan of Program Implementation

Answer: C

Question 60

You are the HNG Program Manager. This program has a $2,345,900 completion budget that is intended to run for two years. At present, the program is 30 percent complete and you have invested $789,000. The program is expected to be 35% complete, but you are slightly behind schedule with some delays. Based on this evidence, how many pennies would the program lose per dollar spent in the work of the program?

A. 15

B. 8

C. 26

D. 11

Answer: D

Question 61

For the organization, you are the program planner. You also built a curriculum that would not only yield things for the company at program completion during the program. Both of the following are components that you will transfer to the company over the life cycle of the program, except for which one?

A. Advantages

B. Consequences of risk assessment

C. Personnel of the program

D. Outputs from creation of teams

Answer: C

Question 62

For your company, you are the program planner and are preparing the program. One of the strategies that you need to develop will determine how you will pass the program's benefits to the organization's activities. What management strategy of the program describes this process?

A. Project of Institutional Transition

B. Program evolution strategy

C. Transfer Plan of Rewards

D. Plan for Program Termination

Answer: B

Question 63

The program has a $1,750,000 BAC that is planned to last for two years. The program is now at its third milestone, which accounts for 35% of the work of the program. As it is, $620,000 of the budget has now been spent on this initiative. Management is worried that since the curriculum may be forty percent complete by this time, the program will still fall on budget. On the basis of this evidence, which sort of output is present in this situation?

A. Schedule, since just $700,000 is the expected benefit of the services.

B. Price, since there is a cost difference in the program of -7,50000

C. Schedule, since there is a schedule performance index of .88 for the program.

D. Price, since the program has an estimate of $1,151,429

to complete.

Answer: C

Question 64

For the organization, you are the program planner. Your latest initiative is to build in your community a modern leisure complex. Franklin, the Chief Executive Officer, is worried with meeting all of the new program's financial and timeline criteria.

Martina, the town's mayor, needs to make sure that safety standards and construction codes are fulfilled by the program. Your boss, Mary Ann, is the Director of the Program and she is worried with the program's start date. Another stakeholder, Hal, is concerned that, when some of the resources are on several initiatives in your scheme, the resources will be stretched thin on the program. In this program, to whom would you report?

A. Hal

B. Mary Ann

C. Franklin

D. Martina

Answer: B

Question 65

When a scope adjustment has been approved, what does a program manager do that will dramatically impact the program costs, assuming that the costs will be applied to the budget of the program?

A. Regulate the baseline cost

B. Transmit the cost of the transition to all stakeholders

C. Adjust the baseline for consistency

D. Transmit the update to all stakeholders

Answer: A

Question 66

As the program manager, part of the job is to coach the project managers about their roles and priorities. Holly, one of the project supervisors, finds it difficult to distinguish the distinction between quality assurance and quality management. She knows that to help you meet the targets of the curriculum, she wants both. Within your program, which assertion best defines quality assurance for a project?

A. Quality assurance is a mechanism powered by inspection in order to avoid defects out of the project.

B. Quality assurance is a mechanism guided by avoidance in order to avoid defects out of the project.

C. Quality assurance determines success and develops priorities for the project team.

D. Quality improvement is an organizational-wide mechanism for doing the job according to the priorities and metrics of the enterprise.

Answer: B

Question 67

You must update any of the following documents anytime a modification reaches your program specifications, except for which one?

A. Job breakdown structure of the curriculum

B. Program Operation List

C. Charter of the Program

D. Scope of program

Answer: C

Question 68

For your company, you are the program planner who uses suppliers from many distinct organizations. An invoice for the job they have done in your program has been submitted by a vendor. You have checked the outcome of the job and conclude with the provider that their contractual task is complete. In response to the vendor's invoice, what do you do next?

A. Accept the payment demand

B. Finalize the report on results

C. Check the Deal

D. Fulfill a financial audit of the job

Answer: A

Question 69

For the organization, you are the program planner. Your system has a budget of $750,000 and one year is anticipated to last. The software is presently 30 percent complete and $245,000 has been invested. At this time, the software is meant to be 40 percent. What is the performance index (SPI) of the timetable for this program?

A. -10%

B. $450

C. $300,000

D. .75

Answer: D

Question 70

For your company, you are the program manager and you are planning to initiate many constituent programs inside the program. In order to complete the project specifications, you need to ensure that each project manager is allowed to use the required project and program tools. For each constituent project in your program, what document do you need to build to ensure that each project manager will access the necessary resources?

A. Charter of project

B. Statement of project scale

C. Document of the project resource specifications

D. Chart of duties and obligations

Answer: A

Question 71

For multiple sectors, an agency funds both services and initiatives. A portfolio, what is it?

A. The cumulative number of funds which have been spent in services, ventures and activities is a portfolio.

B. A portfolio identifies all of the funds invested in the firm.

C. The arrangement of associated initiatives, services, and activities is outlined in a portfolio.

D. A portfolio determines any project or software in a sector or application

Answer: C

Question 72

Joan is her organization's program planner. Management wanted her to build a structured monitoring structure to collect program job detail, threats, improvements, benefits management, and other program aspects. To capture, connect, and document the knowledge management needs, what approach will Joan implement?

A. Modification of control systems

B. Integrated change control management of the software

C. Program management info system

D. Execution of program implementation strategy

Modification of control systems

Answer: C

Question 73

For the organization, you are the program planner. There are eight projects in the new curriculum, which has just begun, and all of the projects share resources like equipment and staff. Management has asked you to decide where inside the software the project tools will be used on each project. They are concerned that any properties will be idle or over-programmed. When the project managers begin sequencing their project operations, what technique would you use to understand the availability of resources?

A. For coordinating tasks, the project managers can use the vital path process.

B. To plan all tasks, the project managers will use PERT.

C. For coordinating tasks, the project managers can use the vital chain process.

D. To plan all tasks, the project managers will create Gantt diagrams.

Answer: C

Question 74

You are the company's program manager and you're trying to decide whether your organization is purchasing or building a tech solution. It'll cost you if you develop the solution, $75,000 to build and it's going to cost you $12,000 to help per month. They will create the solution for $63,000 if you contract a manufacturer, but their solution will cost you $15,500 per month to help you. How many months will you have to use the in-house solution to equal the price of the solution from the vendor?

A. about 6 months

B. You won't be allowed to compare to the charge of the vendor's result.

C. about 3.5 months

D. about 10 months

Answer: C

Question 75

Robert is the NHQ Task's program manager. Before this initiative, his colleagues never interacted for each other, and he is nervous about their potential to become a team in very short order. To promote this process, he would like to build a team building exercise.

Robert would require any of the following details to promote team growth, except for which one?

A. Own records

B. Platform management strategy

C. Risk management plan

D. Drill records

Answer: C

Question 76

What paper asks the seller to include a detailed overview

of a project solution for your project along with a price to finish the project work?

A. Application

B. RFP

C. Proposal

D. Estimate

Answer: A

Question 77

As the project manager, Martha is sharing her perspective on her last project. She claims that they declined to sign after she delivered a formal approval and sign-off contract to the client, saying that their standards were not fulfilled by the goods. What of the following measures may have stopped the situation from taking place? A full solution reflects each correct answer. Choose all that is applicable.

A. Regularly carry out quality checks

B. Sign-off with archiving at major milestones

C. Documenting the needs

D. Completing the project after the timeline

Answer: A,B,C

Question 78

You are the organization's program manager and are focused on compiling the criteria for a new approach and mission statement. In the stakeholder pool, there are some scenarios in which stakeholders and their administrators are asked about future criteria. You are concerned that subordinates may have specifications, proposals, and recommendations to share, but since they do not want to challenge their executives, they do not apply their opinions. Without the partners feeling some fear of retaliation, you think you need a system to collect all specifications. Either one of the following makes it possible for you to collect iteration specifications anonymously and yet encourage all stakeholders to evaluate what has been submitted in an effort to make an agreement?

A. Emphasis Groups

B. Delphi Method

C. Web reviews

D. Workspaces

Answer: B

Question 79

A new software is being contemplated by an organization. The expense of the service is $1,950,000 which will last three years. If it is implemented and the cost of return is six percent, what is the minimum potential benefit that this company should hope to obtain from this program?

A. $3,122,281

B. $2,950,000

C. $1,067,000

D. $2,322,481

Answer: D

Question 80

You are the organization's curriculum planner and you work with some questions concerning the products used in the program. Right now, within ten days, the issues have been allocated to problem owners for resolution. What do you do with the difficulties in the interim?

A. Nothing - any problems with the issues will be handled by the problem owners.

B. Document the questions in the registry of problems.

C. Communicate the state of the concern with the program sponsor.

D. In the vulnerability register, record the problems.

Answer: B

Question 81

In your program, two project administrators, Marcy and Mary, do not agree with the scheduling of project capital and have called for your assistance in deciding the resolution. They fail to talk to each other and each assures you that the other person is preparing project materials that are already set to finish the work for the project. What aspect reflects the conflict of these two project managers in the communication model and their reluctance to communicate about a settlement with each other?

A. Disagreement

B. Uproar

C. Ad hoc

D. Barrier

Answer: C

Question 82

None of the above is responsible for signing off on a project's closing documents?

A. Team members for project

B. Project Director

C. Sponsor

D. Customer

Answer: D

Question 83

You are the NHQ Program manager for your company. There are 14 constituent programs in your program that all build advantages and deliverables for your program.

In your program, you have recently terminated the GHW Project because you have rendered trade-offs with other program programs and the GHW Project's deliverables are no longer affordable. In the GHW project, whose project management operation can take place?

A. Audit of consistency

B. Authentication Scope

C. Regulation of scope

D. Audit of accounts

Answer: B

Question 84

Which one of the below documents sets the project goals?

A. The project charter

B. Schedule

C. company's project chart

D. Project scope statement

Answer: C

Question 85

Who is in charge of preparing the (SOW) statement of work for outsider's project?

A. Client

B. Management group

C. Project Director

D. (CFO)

Answer: A

Question 86

For the organization, you are the program planner. In order to create all of the incentives of the initiative, the new program, which has just been launched, needs to begin many initiatives. In order to initiate the projects inside your software, which document do you need to create?

A. Program Charter

B. Charter of the Program

C. Statement of program spectrum

D. Preliminary Scope Statement Project

Answer: A

Question 87

For the organization, you are the program planner. Starting with yourself, the program planner and the program sponsor, you're now building a transparency matrix.

What method in program administration determines the sponsor of the program?

A. Step of pre-program configuration

B. Authorization of procedures and projects of the software

C. Initiate the process of the program

D. Initiation of the executive committee for the initiative

Answer: C

Question 88

For the organization, you are the program planner. Management has asked you to create a method to monitor the needs, risks, and coordination demands of the program stakeholders. In order to help the program connect more, they would like you to map out each stakeholder or stakeholder group and define themes within the chart. What kind of chart do you build for leadership?

A. Map RACI

B. Analysis map for stakeholders

C. Chart of duties and obligations

D. Matrix of Contact

Answer: B

Question 89

For the organization, you are the program planner. Your curriculum is about to be launched and you are being asked by management for a guide that will describe all the tools, expertise, and competencies that you will use in your program. What paper describes a program's strengths and competencies?

A. Management strategy for staffing

B. Descriptions of the staffing pool

C. Plan of program capital specifications

D. Management strategy for human capital

Answer: A

Question 90

For the company, you are the project manager. The second stage of a seven-phase project has been completed by your project team. Management must review the progress your project team has done at the conclusion of each process to decide if the project can be allowed to proceed. Whose name represents the completion of this method of end-of-phase analysis management for your project?

A. Phase evaluation

B. Audit

C. Quality Assurance

D. Kill point

Answer: D

Question 91

A byproduct that you could market to a consumer is generated by the software. The cost of the by-product would cover the program's cost by about $7,500 a month. Is this an indication of a constructive reaction to risk?

A. Sharing of

B. Reinforce

C. Accepting

D. Exploiting

Answer: D

Question 92

You are your company's program manager and management wants you to identify how you will make decisions in the planning processes of the program. What document for program management should serve as the basis for all future decisions on the program?

A. Program budget

B. Program management plan

C. Statement of program scope

D. Program requirements

Answer: C

Question 93

What is the % of nonverbal communication?

A. 30%

B. 80%

C. 55%

D. 42%

Answer: A

Question 94

You are the program manager of the JNH Program. Tom, a project manager in your program, has just completed his project and is ready to officially close his project. You agree that Tom's project is completed. What role do you play in Tom's project closure?

A. You have to ensure that the sponsor of the project closes the project.

B. You must ensure that, at the project stage, the programs within the program are closed.

C. Before the project's activities close, you must close the project.

D. For the project manager, you would guarantee that the program management committee closes the project.

Answer: B

Question 95

Which one of the following is NOT an element of the process of risk monitoring and control?

A. Executing plans for risk response

B. Completing detailed risk evaluation

C. Tracking the threats found

D. Determining what new threats have emerged

Answer: B

Question 96

For the organization, you are the program planner. Your program has recently completed the breadth of the program and you have passed the rewards to the organization's operations. You must complete certain forms and procedures as required by your company before your software is deemed closed. The specifications for completing the documents and reports are also known as what?

A. Program managerial closure

B. Organization environmental effects

C. Closing procedures

D. enterprise progression assets

Answer: B

Question 97

A knowledge area defines a subset of program management and its processes within that domain. For example, the knowledge area of quality management includes the processes related directly to quality management only. What knowledge field guarantees that all fields of knowledge communicate with each other correctly?

A. Platform aids management

B. Program management development

C. Interaction management

D. Integration management

Answer: D

Question 98

You're the HYH Program Planner for your company. Your program is to build a new sports arena within 12 months for your area. There are seven projects in your program and you've worked with all of the project managers before. And if you worked with project managers before establishing the authority of the project managers and their projects, you do need to. The text does the project manager call for the project?

A. Development management

B. Program HR management idea

C. Project charter for each project

D. PM charter

Answer: C

Question 99

In order to decide the vendor to purchase from, you are the software manager for your business and compare the sellers. You have built a histogram in your study to show each seller the pros and cons. For each vendor, you've generated five importance categories and allocated values to each category. Your five classifications are:

Costs

Timetable

Experience that is

Certifications

Guarantee

Each segment has a separate point value and the contract will be won by the vendor who earns the most points in total. What kind of assessment of the seller are you conducting?

A. Monte Carlo simulation

B. Proficient decision

C. Benchmarking

D. Measured scoring model

Answer: C

Question 100

The software for Kelly is sliding in its timeline. Management is concerned that the software will be late and that fines and fees will cost the company several thousand dollars. They also asked Kelly to use a compression method for the remainder of the timetable that would help the program end on time. However, the system that Kelly can use does not add costs to the software. In this case, what period compression technique should Kelly use?

A. Smash the program

B. Include start time to the program

C. hasten the program

D. reduce the program agenda

Answer: C